ARCTIC
TALE

COMPANION TO THE
MAJOR MOTION PICTURE

ARCTIC
TALE

BY BARRY VARELA

BASED ON THE MOTION PICTURE
NARRATION WRITTEN BY
LINDA WOOLVERTON AND
MOSE RICHARDS AND KRISTIN GORE

NATIONAL GEOGRAPHIC

WASHINGTON, D.C.

Arctic Tale has been created from the best Arctic wildlife cinematography of
the past decade. Nanu and Seela are composite characters whose lives are
based upon material shot throughout the Arctic over many years. Their stories
represent the real conditions polar bears and walruses face today.

The events, characters, entities and/or firms depicted in this motion picture
and book are fictitious. Any similarity to actual events or persons, living or
dead, or to actual entities or firms is purely coincidental.

Insert photo credits: 1 up: Norbert Rosing / NGS; 1 lo: Paul Nicklen/ NGS;
2 up: Norbert Rosing / NGS; 2 lo left: Brian Skerry; 2 lo right: Norbert Rosing / NGS;
3 up left: Karen Kasmauski/ NGS; 3 up right: Paul Nicklen/ NGS;
3 lo: Norbert Rosing / NGS; 4: Paul Nicklen/ NGS

Paperback ISBN: 978-1-4263-0106-3
Library edition ISBN: 978-1-4263-0107-0

Library of Congress Cataloging in Publication information
available upon request.

Printed in the U.S.A.

A REAL ADVENTURE
IN THE COOLEST PLACE ON EARTH

PARAMOUNT CLASSICS PRESENTS A NATIONAL GEOGRAPHIC FILMS PRODUCTION "ARCTIC TALE" AS TOLD BY QUEEN LATIFAH
MUSIC BY JOBY TALBOT MUSIC SUPERVISOR FRANKIE PINE EXECUTIVE MUSIC PRODUCER DAVID BEAL EMMETT MALLOY RALPH SALL PRODUCED BY KATTIE EVANS CHRIS MILLER
EDITORS TIM KELLY JOHN BARD MANULIS MICHAEL ROSENFELD PRODUCED BY ADAM LEIPZIG KEENAN SMART
NARRATION WRITTEN BY LINDA WOOLVERTON AND MOSE RICHARDS AND KRISTIN GORE DIRECTED BY ADAM RAVETCH & SARAH ROBERTSON

GROUP SALES 1-866-397-6339

AS TOLD BY QUEEN LATIFAH   ARCTICTALEMOVIE.COM

ARCTIC
TALE

CHAPTER ONE

Nanu sniffs the warm air inside the ice cave. Above her, through the small opening at the top of the cave, she sees a disc of blue light. It is a glimpse of the outside world—a world Nanu has never ventured into. Though she is four months old, she has never left the safety of the maternal cave.

Nanu yawns and stretches, snuggling against the soft, warm bulk of her mother.

Pressing her paws against her mother's belly, Nanu finds the nipple. She tastes the sweet, rich, warm milk, the only food she has ever known. Drowsily, Nanu nurses, then closes her eyes. Her mother licks the top of her head gently, and Nanu falls into a deep, contented sleep. Even her brother's playful shoves can't wake her.

Four months earlier, in December, when Nanu and her brother were born, they were blind. After a few weeks, their eyes opened, though there wasn't much to see. During the long Arctic winter, the sun never rises above the horizon. Even at noontime, the sky is a dusky purple, and you can see the stars. Inside a polar bear cave, it's pitch black.

But Nanu could smell her mother and her brother. She could hear her mother grunting and yawning, and she could hear her brother whining when he was tired or hungry. Although she couldn't see, she knew she wasn't alone.

After a short nap, Nanu awakes. It is mid-April—springtime—and the sun is over the horizon for more than half the day.

Light streams in through the cave opening, reflecting off the icy walls. The inside of the cave shines milky blue. Nanu can see her mother and brother clearly, their black eyes and black noses set off from their bright white faces.

The breeze coming in through the cave opening is cool and full of promise.

Nanu peers up at the blue above. She sniffs at the breeze. What's out there? She feels an urge to go exploring.

Her brother playfully nips at one of Nanu's ears, but she ignores him. Digging into the icy slope with her strong front claws, Nanu clambers toward the light.

Losing her grip, she slides back, bumping into her mother.

Her mother swings her head around to see what Nanu is doing, grunts, and uses her nose to nudge Nanu forward. Nanu digs her claws into the icy slope and starts back up.

Since entering the cave in November, Nanu's mother has had nothing to eat or drink. Polar bears don't hibernate the same way animals like groundhogs, bats, and frogs do. In those animals, body functions slow down and body temperature falls.

Polar bear mothers, by contrast, simply fall into a very deep sleep—so deep, in fact, that they don't wake up even when the cubs are being born.

No food, no drink—Nanu's mother

hasn't even peed since last fall! She is as
ready as Nanu to leave the cave.

Nudged on by her mother, Nanu scrambles to the lip of the cave opening. Poking
her black nose through the hole, she sniffs
deeply. The air is sharp and crisp—completely
unlike the air inside the cave, which is warm
and heavy with the smell of bear.

Nanu edges forward till her whole head
is outside the cave. She blinks and squints in
the bright sunlight. The wind whips across
her face, buffeting her ears. As her eyes get
used to the light, Nanu looks around. She
takes in the landscape—blue sky above and
white ice below. Snow swirls in the wind.
In the far distance, Nanu sees a sliver of blue
ocean on the horizon.

Such a world—of cold wind, snow, ice,
and seawater—may seem forbidding, but to

Nanu it is perfect. Hundreds of thousands of years of evolution have resulted in the polar bear's perfect adaptation to this harsh environment. Nanu is fit to live in a world of ice and snow. The far north is all she knows, and all she will ever know. It is her Arctic home.

In the sliver of blue ocean that Nanu can see from the slope of her birthplace, another animal has just been born. Seela, a baby walrus, is only a few minutes old, but already she's swimming like an expert.

Walrus mothers give birth in the spring, in a maze of ice floes that serves as a protected nursery. Unlike polar bear cubs, who are tiny, blind, and helpless when first born, walrus calves weigh over 80 pounds (over 35 kilograms) at birth and can see well.

Seela's mother grips her newborn calf between her flippers. The two walruses, mother and child, press their noses together. Seela's sensitive whiskers brush against her mother's snout and whiskers. For a long moment, Seela touches her mother's face, taking in its shape. Seela breathes in, inhaling her mother's scent. Her mother grunts, growls quietly, gives a little bark. Seela is memorizing her mother's face, odor, and sound. She will remember them for the rest of her life.

Only a few hours old, Seela trails her umbilical cord behind her as she zooms through the water. Beating the water with her front flippers, using her back flippers as a rudder, she darts and swerves and spins

through the icy water. Above her, chunks
of ice several feet (over a meter) thick glow
with a spectral greenish blue. Seela turns a
somersault, then returns to the surface for air.

Seela's mother bobs up beside her, and
Seela ducks under the surface. The two
swim leisurely, Seela nursing. Like Nanu,
Seela survives solely on her mother's milk
for the first months of life.

When Seela is full, she swims to the
surface. Nap time! Bobbing upright in the
water, Seela's mother holds Seela between
her flippers as she sleeps. Feeling tired
herself, Seela's mother takes in a great breath
of air, filling the two pockets on either side
of her throat. These inflatable "balloons"
keep her body upright and her head above
water even as she sleeps. Seela's mother
nods off.

As the two walruses snooze, a third walrus approaches—another female, fully mature like Seela's mother but without a calf of her own. Seela's mother wakes and gives a short, friendly bark of greeting. The female nuzzles Seela's mother, then sniffs Seela. Seela wakes and presses her whiskers to the newcomer's face.

For the next three years, this female will stay with Seela's mother and help care for and protect Seela. She will act as a sort of "auntie" to Seela.

Seela's mother grunts and dives under the water. Seela and Auntie follow close behind as Seela's mother leads them to a nearby ice floe. While Auntie watches for predators such as orcas, Seela's mother shows Seela how to get out of the water and onto the ice. It's the first thing a baby walrus needs to learn. If Seela can't get out of the water, she'll eventually get too cold and drown.

But when it comes to getting out of the water, Seela's mother has an advantage. She's got long, sharp, strong tusks. She plunges them into the ice, hauling her body up.

Seela, meanwhile, tries to flop up onto the ice floe but slides back down into the water. Seela's mother dives back into the sea and shows her again how to get up onto the ice. Seela tries, but the ice is slippery, and she is tired.

At her mother's urging, Seela finally hauls herself up onto the ice, where she can rest. The air temperature is 20 below zero Fahrenheit (30 below Celsius), and she's lying on a block of ice, but it's still warmer than being in that frigid water.

Seela's mother and Auntie join her in

basking on the floe, and the trio fall asleep. For Seela, it's been a long and exhausting first day of life.

CHAPTER TWO

Meanwhile, Nanu and her brother scamper around the mouth of their snow cave on Snow Mountain. They take flying leaps and tackle each other. They rear up on their hind legs, knock each other over, and wrestle, tumbling over and over. This rough play prepares them for later in life, when they will hunt down prey.

Though she's hungry from her long confinement in the cave, Nanu's mother takes the time to enjoy her newfound freedom. She slides down an icy slope and rolls around in loose snow. The wind ruffles her shaggy white fur.

When she notices that her cubs have wandered too far away, she gives a loud, barking call. The cubs come running. The polar bear family isn't straying too far away from the ice cave just yet. In fact, Nanu's brother isn't paying attention to where he is, takes a step back, and drops down into the cave. Nanu dives in right after him, to continue their wrestling match.

After 12 days, Nanu's mother leads the cubs away from the snow cave. Not having eaten in almost six months, Nanu's mother is extremely hungry. The hunting grounds are down the mountain, on the ice shelf that extends for miles out over the sea.

Nanu and her brother stay close to their mother's side as they begin their journey to the hunting grounds. The cubs don't even look back as they leave their birthplace.

They are so intent on their journey that they don't notice another creature following at a safe distance behind them—an arctic fox. In the frozen north, there isn't a lot a predator the size of a fox can catch. Birds can fly away, and most seals are too big. Only seal pups are small enough for the fox to kill.

But when polar bears catch seals, they often eat only the blubber, leaving the meat and organs behind. Even when they eat more of the kill, there's always something left over. So a polar bear will frequently have a little companion fox that trails it wherever it goes, feeding off the table scraps.

Polar bears are at the top of the Arctic food chain. They have no natural enemies—they hunt, but aren't hunted. Nothing can kill a polar bear—except another polar bear.

And the tracks of another polar bear are just what Nanu's mother spots in the snow. She chuffs and grunts, letting the cubs know that something has upset her. They prick up their ears, alert.

Nanu's mother spots a full-grown male bear in the distance. Though the male poses little threat to her, Nanu's mother knows that given a chance he will kill her cubs—not to eat, but in order to cut down on the competition.

She gives out a loud, high-pitched shriek, which the cubs recognize instinctively as the alarm call. Nanu's mother turns and runs away from the male bear, and the cubs dash off behind her, straining to keep up.

The male hears the alarm call, turns, and spots the polar bear family. He charges after them, but he soon gives up the chase. They are too far away, and he is too hungry. He's more interested in hunting prey than in catching a couple of cubs that he wouldn't even eat.

Though male polar bears are the largest land predators in the world—twice the size of female polar bears—he knows that the mother will fight him to defend her cubs. It's easier to move on and look for something that doesn't fight back.

He sniffs at the wind. Polar bears have extremely sensitive noses and can smell prey up to 40 miles (64 kilometers) away. The bear rears up on his hind legs to get a better sniff at the wind. He stands ten feet tall and weighs over 1,500 pounds (700 kilograms)—as much as ten full-grown men. His front paws are enormous—almost 6 inches (15 centimeters) long and 9 inches (23 centimeters) wide—and come equipped with powerful, dagger-sharp curved claws.

The bear sniffs again. He's caught the scent of something. He trots across the ice toward the open ocean, toward the source of the scent.

In the water, Seela twirls and dives, gliding between and beneath chunks of ice. Smaller bits of ice swirl in her wake. Seela surfaces, blowing warm air through her nostrils, like a miniature whale spouting. Though she's only a few days old, the thick

layer of blubber under her wrinkly brown
skin keeps her warm in the icy water.

At the edge of the ice sheet, the male
polar bear plunges into the water. He, too,
has a thick layer of fat beneath his skin to
insulate him from the cold.

Though not born to the ocean like
walruses, polar bears are excellent swimmers
and can travel miles through the water.

Paddling steadily, the male polar bear
makes his way toward Seela and her family.

Unaware of the approaching danger,
Seela bobs in the water near her mother.

Auntie patrols nearby, ever watchful of predators.

The male bear's white head cuts through the surface of the water for an instant as he takes a breath and sniffs out his prey. In that moment, Auntie catches sight of the bear and bellows in alarm.

Seela and her mother turn and flee, swimming underwater as fast as they can.

The bear dives underwater, too, in quick pursuit. But Auntie is there to block his way. Though the bear is armed with razor-sharp teeth and claws, Auntie attacks. She's much heavier than he is, and she's in her native element—the water. A polar bear is no match for an angry walrus in the open ocean. Auntie slashes at him with her foot-long tusks. The bear evades her tusks, but he knows this is a fight he can't win.

The male polar bear turns back toward the ice shelf. Auntie bellows triumphantly. Safe now, Seela and her mother stop fleeing and rejoin Auntie. The little family all touch noses in reunion.

On the ice shelf, the male polar bear shakes himself, throwing water in every direction. He's given up on a meal of walrus—for now.

CHAPTER THREE

Seela dozes, snuggled between her mother and Auntie on an ice floe. With them on the ice are dozens of other walruses—mothers with their young, plus all their aunties and sisters and grandmothers and nieces.

Walruses gather in herds ranging in size from several dozen individuals on a small ice floe to great gatherings of thousands all crowded together on the ice shelf. During the summer, the females live separately from the males.

Within the herd, the biggest females with the biggest tusks get first choice of where to lie down. And the best place to lie? Right in the center of the herd, surrounded by all that glorious walrus flesh.

Seela's mother and Auntie are two of the larger females, so Seela has a prime spot near the center of the ice floe. She can't move without touching her mother, Auntie, or some other high-ranking female. She can feel the warmth of their bodies, hear them snuffing and sneezing and farting, smell their bodies and breaths.

She runs her sensitive whiskers across the broad expanse of her mother's belly, searching for the nipple. Seela nurses, then rolls over to snuggle against Auntie. A breeze keeps her comfortably cool. She drapes herself across Auntie's fat warm neck, burps, and closes her eyes.

On the ice sheet, Nanu's mother is hunting seals. Ringed seals live mostly in the ocean near the pack ice, where they hunt shrimp, lobsters, and fish such as cod.

Working from below, a ringed seal will use its strong, sharp claws to dig a hole through the ice to the air above. The seal uses the hole to come up for air after diving for shrimp or fish. The seal will use several breathing holes, maintaining them through the winter so they don't freeze over. The seal will also dig out a burrow in a snow drift near one of the holes, to sleep and rest in.

Nanu's mother hunts for ringed seals using two methods. The first method involves simply waiting near a breathing hole, The bear must wait very patiently and without moving, so the seal doesn't know it's there. When the seal pops its head out of the water, the bear dives in headfirst after it. Seal dinner!

The other way a polar bear can catch a seal is by trapping it in its burrow in the snow.

Nanu's mother sniffs at the snow near a breathing hole. Even though the seal may be covered by several feet of snow, Nanu's mother can pick up her scent.

Nanu and her brother watch as their mother snuffles her nose through the snow, trying to locate the seal. She moves slowly, carefully, quietly, not wanting to alert the seal that she's sneaking up on her.

When Nanu's mother has found the seal, she rises up on her hind legs and comes down hard with both front paws on the snow. She crashes through the several feet of snow and ice to the hollowed-out seal burrow below. The seal desperately wiggles and squirms, trying to evade the bear.

This time the seal gets away. It slithers through the burrow, back to its breathing hole, where it dives into the water and swims swiftly away.

Nanu's mother shakes the snow from her fur. More often than not, the hunt fails. But when she does succeed, the result is a seal feast for her and her cubs—and for the little arctic fox who's always nearby.

During spring, Nanu's mother will succeed in killing a seal every five or six days.

The hunting is so good that Nanu and her family will eat only the blubber and skin, leaving the muscle and organs to be devoured by scavengers.

Out in the open ocean, the walrus herd is preparing for a hunt of its own. With those long, sharp tusks, walruses must take on some large, fierce, vicious creatures—or so you might think.

The walrus herd scans the seafloor, searching for landmarks the elder members remember from the last time they hunted this part of the ocean, five years before.

One walrus spots a section of whale backbone, decaying slowly in the icy waters. Another sees an unusual, pointy boulder.

Using clues such as these, the herd
approaches its prey...

Clams! Thousands upon thousands
of them.

Head down, a walrus feels along the
ocean floor with its sensitive whiskers,
searching for clams. When a clam is found,
the walrus beats at it with its front flippers
to knock it loose, or spits a jet of water at it.
Catching the loose clamshell with its mouth,
the walrus then sucks the juicy clam out.

Each dive can last ten minutes, and in
that time a walrus can devour 60 clams.

The herd's clam hunt will last three days,
and in that time each walrus will eat over
4,000 clams. Baby Seela watches her mother
and Auntie as they hunt, but she doesn't
eat any clams herself. Seela's still living on
mother's milk.

After the big clam hunt, the herd sleeps off the meal on an ice floe. The walruses let their digestive systems go to work, and the sounds of walrus belches and farts echo across the water.

Seela's not bothered by the racket, though. She's drunk her fill, and now she's snuggled tight against her mother, fast asleep.

On the ice sheet, Nanu, her brother, and her mother are also enjoying full bellies. Springtime, when the ringed seals are plentiful, is prime hunting season for polar bears. During these months adult bears fatten up for the summer, when the pack ice disappears and seals become much harder to catch.

Nanu and her brother eat seal, but they also still nurse. Polar bear cubs drink their mother's milk until the age of two.

As spring turns to summer, the sun stays in the sky for more and more hours of the day, until night disappears altogether.

The sun never rises very high in the sky, however. It stays just above the horizon, traveling in a great circle all the way around every 24 hours. Relative to the winter, the Arctic summer is balmy. Temperatures climb above freezing, at times reaching above 50 degrees Fahrenheit (10 degrees Celsius).

The sun heats the seawater, causing microscopic algae to bloom. With the algae comes an explosion of life—jellyfish, shrimp, plankton—that feeds on the plants. These creatures in turn draw larger animals that have migrated north to join in the summer feast—fish such as herring and salmon, birds such as the arctic tern and the snowy owl, bowhead whales, harbor porpoises, orcas. The ocean and the sky teem with life.

With the coming of summer, the pack ice breaks up. With loud snaps and booms, cracks appear in the surface of the ice. Huge sections of the sheet heave and shudder, as the seawater underneath lifts and shifts them about.

Nanu and her family wait out the warm summer months, unable to catch seals without the hard pack ice but trusting that with autumn the ice will return.

The days soon get shorter. By the time fall comes, the sun is in the sky for only 12 hours a day, and even at noon, it is barely above the horizon. Temperatures drop, and the ice begins to re-form, starting from the rock coast and spreading into the open water.

Nanu's mother shows her cubs how to rear up and pounce down. Proper hunting technique will be critical for their survival as adults.

Nanu practices pouncing. She's getting better at it. Her brother? Not so much. His practice consists mainly of rolling around in the snow.

The weeks pass and the days grow ever shorter. The temperature has fallen, but not as much as in previous years. The ice sheet is thinner, and it doesn't reach as far out into the ocean, either. Nanu's mother has lived through a dozen previous autumns, but she's never before seen the ice so meager.

Without a thick layer of ice, the ringed seals won't make their breathing holes and burrows. No ringed seals means no food.

For Nanu and her family, the summer fast has turned into a fall fast. Luckily, polar bears can enter a sort of "walking hibernation," in which their body functions slow down. Nanu's mother won't starve, and Nanu and her brother can still live off their mother's milk.

Finally, three months late, the pack ice forms, and Nanu's mother can go hunting.

She spots a ringed seal and her pup on the surface of the ice. Normally, the ringed seal mother would have dug out a burrow and kept her pup beneath the snow. But this year, the ice formed so late, and so thinly, that the seal had no burrow.

Nanu's mother approaches the seal family. Her usual hunting technique would be to sniff out their burrow, then pounce on them in surprise. But since the seals are out in the open, there's no way she can surprise them.

All she can do is rush at them. The seals, of course, dive into their nearby breathing hole. Nanu's mother leaps in after them, but the seals are too quick. They escape, and Nanu's mother goes hungry.

The little arctic fox that follows them is disappointed by Nanu's mother's failure. He's getting pretty hungry too.

Nanu's mother is growing desperate. It's been almost six months since she's had a meal. She leads her cubs across the thin, half-frozen ice sheet, searching for ringed seals. She can't find any.

A flock of birds wheels in the sky near the polar bear family. Nanu's mother knows that where there are birds, there must be other animals as well. She heads off in the direction of the birds, with Nanu and her brother close behind.

Sure enough, they come across a freshly killed seal. The predator, a huge male polar bear, dozes in the snow nearby. He hasn't noticed them approach.

Driven by hunger, Nanu's mother tears at the seal carcass. She picks out the fattiest, most satisfying bits. The cubs join in the meal, biting off chunks of flesh with their sharp teeth. The meat is still warm.

The male polar bear opens an eye and realizes that three invaders are taking his kill. He rouses himself, barks furiously, and rushes toward Nanu and her family.

Nanu's mother screams in alarm, and she and the cubs turn tail and rush off. The male bear pursues them for a short distance, then halts. He bellows after them.

Nanu's mother chanced death to gain a little meal, but the risk was worth it. She has some food in her belly and is feeling stronger.

And just in the nick of time. Out over the ocean, a blizzard is forming, and the storm is moving shoreward fast.

The sea has turned an angry gray-green color. Wind whips the tops off whitecaps and pushes the water into enormous, 15-foot (3-meter) swells. Snow swirls down, ice chunks are tossed about, and the boundary between water and sky becomes blurred.

The walrus herd bobs in the water, riding out the storm. They try to stick together for safety, but giant waves crash down, separating them.

Seela works her flippers, trying to stay close to her mother and Auntie. Strong currents pull her away from them, and she ducks underwater to swim back. When she comes up for air, she can't see them through the driving snow and wind-whipped froth.

Seela barks, and she hears, far off in the distance, the faint barking replies of her mother and Auntie. She dives under a swell, and when she comes back up, she barks again. This time she hears no reply.

She has become separated from the herd.

On the pack ice, Nanu and her mother and brother huddle against the wind. The temperature has dropped to 40 below zero Fahrenheit (also 40 below zero Celsius)—

not dangerous for a polar bear. But the wind buffets them at 80 miles (130 kilometers) an hour, and they are all weakened from the lack of food over the previous months.

Nanu's mother trudges forward, head lowered, into the wind. Nanu and her brother stay close beside her, using her bulk as shelter from the gale. Nanu's mother grunts, and the cubs give small grunts in reply.

Moving onward, Nanu's mother grunts again, but this time only Nanu replies. Her brother has fallen behind.

Nanu's mother turns to check on her cub. He stumbles forward, crying. Nanu and her mother return to him. Nanu's mother nuzzles his face with hers. She licks his nose. He takes a few more steps, and then his hind legs give way abruptly.

Nanu gives him a gentle nudge with her nose, but he can't get up. He bleats quietly then lies down in the snow and closes his eyes. He's too exhausted to go on.

The wind howls, and the snow swirls all around them.

Nanu's mother lies down next to her son. Her body heat will help keep him warm as he rests. Nanu lies down next to him too.

All that Nanu and her mother can do is wait. Wait for Nanu's brother to regain his strength. Wait for the blizzard to let up.

In the ocean, the storm has moved out. The snow has stopped, the wind has eased, and the waters have calmed.

The walrus herd bobs on the swells. But one young calf is missing. Seela.

Seela's mother and Auntie call for her— long, searching, plaintive howls. They receive no response.

They circle the herd, desperately looking for Seela, calling out for her. They sniff the air, trying to catch her scent. The sea rises and falls, and Seela's mother and Auntie ride the swells, looking around. They don't see her.

Nanu's brother lies on the ice, his eyes closed. The storm is over, and a thin layer of snow blankets his white fur. His breathing is shallow, his chest barely rising and falling.

Nanu nudges at him gently with her

black nose, but he doesn't respond. Nanu
whines quietly.

Nanu's mother shifts her weight and
turns to sniff her cubs. She and Nanu touch
noses. Then she licks Nanu's brother on the
forehead. His eyes remain closed.

Nanu's mother growls sadly.

Seela bobs in the swells. For the first time
in her life, she is all alone. She doesn't know
where the herd is. She doesn't know where
the ice sheet is. She is lost.

There are no ice floes nearby for her to
clamber onto, to get out of the chilly water.
Though her thick blubber can protect her
from the cold for long periods of time, and
though she can sleep while in the water,

Nanu and her mother, not far from the cave on Snow Mountain.

Seela and her mother on an ice floe, surrounded by family.

The herd tries to crowd onto an ice floe that's just too small.

A ringed seal.

An arctic fox cub.

Nesting murres.　　The male polar bear is the Arctic's top predator.

Nanu with her mother and brother.

The Arctic—so full of life—is changing rapidly. The loss of the great ice sheets threatens all of the creatures that make this vast northern expanse their home.

eventually she must climb out. If she doesn't, she will tire, grow cold, and die.

Seela closes her eyes, her little old-man's face showing weariness. Cold seawater sloshes over her nostrils.

Just then she hears something—a bark, far off in the distance.

Her mother's bark!

Seela opens her large brown eyes and barks back, over and over.

She hears another bark, louder this time. Auntie!

Auntie and her mother swim up to her, and Seela chortles with happiness. Auntie hugs her with her big front flippers, and Seela's mother nuzzles her face.

Seela rubs her whiskers over the familiar contours of her mother's and her Auntie's faces. Then she ducks underwater to nurse.

Her mother's warm, fatty milk fills Seela's belly. She can feel her strength returning.

After a few minutes, the three walruses start swimming in the direction of the herd. Auntie leads the way. She has to swim fast to keep ahead of Seela.

The little pup is in a hurry to rejoin the herd.

Nanu's mother is hungry. If she is to live and continue to take care of Nanu, she must resume the hunt.

Nanu sniffs at her brother. His body is cold. Nanu looks up at her mother.

Nanu's mother whines gently and paws at her cub. He doesn't move.

Slowly Nanu's mother turns away. She has to hunt now. She must leave Nanu's brother behind.

Nanu follows her mother. A breeze stirs across the ground. It covers Nanu's brother's body with a light layer of snow.

CHAPTER FOUR

Winter passes, then spring, summer, and fall—another year of seasons with the eternal rhythms of the Arctic— the spring algae bloom, the ice melt of summer, the freeze of fall, and the dark of winter.

As the seasons pass, the walrus herd migrates to follow the ice. Walruses prefer to live on the edge of the pack ice, where they have easy access to both open water and solid surfaces of ice. During fall and winter, as the ice sheet expands, the herd moves south. In spring and summer, as the ice retreats, the herd moves north.

For the past few years, however, the ice has expanded more slowly and contracted more quickly. The herd's migration has come earlier in the spring and later in the fall.

In years past, by following the edge of the pack ice as it moved south in the spring and moved north in the fall, the herd would migrate a thousand miles (1,600 kilometers) each way. Lately the migratory distance has been less than half that.

Seela, now almost two years old, has begun to sprout little tusks. Though she now weighs about 600 pounds (about 300 kilograms), she stays by her mother's and Auntie's sides. She is still dependent on them for guidance and protection, and she still drinks her mother's milk.

Seela has begun to notice walruses outside her all-female herd, however. She has heard male voices singing, courting the older females who are ready to mate.

The males' love songs are extremely complicated and take years for young walruses to learn. The songs consist of a sequence of pings, creaks, pops, bell-like gonging sounds, knocks, taps—all produced in the walruses' throats.

There are two songs—a long version and a short version. There are minor variations in the way individuals sing the songs, but basically all males learn both songs, and the songs remain the same from year to year, passed down from generation to generation.

Swimming near a herd of females, the males will sing the songs over and over, for days at a time, trying to woo the females. Sound travels easily through water, and a swimming female can hear songs coming from miles away.

The females can even hear the songs when they are lounging on ice floes. The songs' vibrations penetrate the ice and are broadcast into the air.

During the winter mating season, the sound of the males' love songs is the females' constant companion.

Though Seela is too young to mate, she is already learning to judge which males are the best singers and therefore the best potential mates.

At two years old, Nanu has grown as well, and, like Seela, she is still dependent on her mother. Nanu has learned how to hunt, and her diet consists largely of the seals she and her mother catch.

Nanu still nurses a little, and she stays as close to her mother's side as she did when she first emerged from the maternal cave.

Spring—high hunting season for polar bears—has come early to the north this year. The ice sheet, which failed to extend as far out into the open water as in years past, is melting earlier and faster this year. Seals are harder to find, and the hunting has been difficult.

Nanu's mother knows that she can no longer hunt for two. If this were a normal year, Nanu might stay with her mother through the end of the spring hunting season, then set out on her own. But this year is far from normal. Nanu's mother is forced to do something a little earlier than usual.

She and Nanu are making their way together across a broad expanse of ice in search of ringed seal breathing holes. It's been many days since they've come across one.

Nanu's mother turns to Nanu, lowers her head, and growls low and long in the back of her throat. It is a warning growl—not a warning of outside danger, but a warning of hostility.

Nanu's mother glares at her daughter. Nanu sees something in her mother's eyes that she's never seen before. Her mother is driving her away.

Nanu must set off on her own now so that both she and her mother will have a better chance to survive in the changing conditions of the Arctic.

Nanu whimpers and attempts to approach her mother.

Her mother growls louder and bristles.

Nanu understands. She must leave now. She turns and trots away quickly, before her mother chooses to chase her away.

Polar bears live solitary lives, with pairs forming only during the brief late-fall mating season. Mothers stay with their cubs for only a little more than two years.

Nanu may never see her mother again. And if she does, they will greet each other like strangers.

For most of the rest of her life, Nanu will wander the Arctic alone.

Well, not quite alone.

A little fox trails behind her at a safe distance, ever hopeful of a free meal.

CHAPTER FIVE

E arlier than in past years, summer warmth envelopes the Arctic.

Icicles form on the lips of hollowed-out snow drifts as the ice melts and drips. The ice sheet has broken up into a sea of slushy ice chunks, and ringed seals are nowhere to be found.

Nanu picks her way across the unsteady ice, jumping from patch to small, crumbly patch. Sometimes the ice chunks shift and turn under her weight, dumping her into the sea. That's okay—Nanu can swim to the next tippy chunk of ice.

The arctic fox can't swim. But of course he weighs much less than Nanu does, and he doesn't tip the ice patch over. He leaps lightly across the ice, keeping up with Nanu. Without a polar bear to catch seals for him, the fox won't starve, but scavenging from Nanu's catch is easier than making a living off small prey and the sparse Arctic vegetation.

Nanu isn't starving yet, but she's getting awfully hungry. Hopping and swimming across the fractured ice field, Nanu encounters an enormous flock of thick-billed murres. There are hundreds of thousands of birds in the flock, and though Nanu has never before attempted to catch such small prey, hunger drives her to try.

The black-and-white birds look a bit like penguins (which live at the South Pole and which Nanu has never seen). Unlike penguins, murres can fly, though they're not very good at flying in the air. What they are better designed to do is "fly" through the water, in pursuit of fish and other prey. Flapping their wings and using their webbed feet as rudders, they dart through the water like swallows through the air.

Nanu paddles, her head above water, toward a likely looking group of murres. The birds see her coming and duck beneath the surface. Nanu dives, too, hoping to catch one. Though she swims as fast as she can, the birds are much too quick and elusive for her. She doesn't even come close to snagging a meal—and even if she had, a little bony bird could never be a good substitute for a plump, tender ringed seal.

Coming up for air, Nanu learns that she isn't the only large creature in the sea. Nearby she sees a long, sharp, bony spear rise slowly out of the water, followed by the rounded face of a narwhal.

A narwhal is a type of small whale. The males (and a few rare females) have a very unusual feature—a single, very long spiral tusk that projects out from the upper left jaw. A narwhal's tusk is sensitive to temperature, moisture, and salt, and the animal uses it to "taste" the air and sea. Narwhals eat cod and other fish, as well as shrimp and squid.

Full-grown polar bears will sometimes attack a narwhal, especially a youngster or an old, weakened one. The fatty flesh and blubber of a whale would make an ideal feast for Nanu. But these narwhals are all full grown, and Nanu herself is not. She's no match for these whales that are about ten times her weight.

Nanu hauls herself out of the water onto an ice floe then shakes herself. She is hungry, and another day has passed with nothing to eat. Pack ice is nowhere to be found, and neither are the seal breathing holes and burrows that polar bears depend on for hunting.

Nanu barks in frustration.

Half a mile away, the arctic fox yips and whines in answer. Open ocean separates the fox from Nanu, and as the polar bear drifts away on her floe, the fox paws at the edge of his own little chunk of ice. His whole way of life is about to change.

The fox is losing his polar bear companion. Like Nanu, from now on he'll be on his own.

Farther out at sea, the walrus herd crowds onto the few remaining ice rafts. Usually walruses are content to pile up on top of each other, but not in these circumstances. The air is warm and uncomfortable, and there isn't enough ice for everybody.

Tempers flare, and a large, ill-mannered walrus jabs her tusks into the side of her neighbor. The second cow bellows in anger and returns the jab in kind.

The scuffle spreads through the herd. Tusks lash out, some drawing blood. The walruses bark and chuff at one another. One unfortunate walrus comes down at the wrong angle on her neighbor and snaps a tusk in half.

Finally, fed up by the fighting, one walrus at the edge of the floe plunges into the water. It's the signal everyone's been waiting for. Every walrus makes a dash for the water, leaving the shrinking ice floe behind.

There isn't enough ice for all of the walruses to crowd onto, and they can't stay in the water indefinitely. Hungry polar bears, frustrated by the dearth of ringed seals, patrol the nearby shore. The walruses can't move there. They'll have to set out across the open seas in search of a new home.

Seela stays close to her mother and Auntie. The open ocean, with its sharks and orcas, isn't the safest place for a young walrus. Seela barks, and her mother and

Auntie answer. The three touch noses. Then Seela's mother dips under the waves and sets out swimming along with the rest of the herd. Seela and Auntie follow close behind.

In the fractured ice field, Nanu has reached a desperation point. She is hungry and growing weak. There are no seals to hunt. She is too big and slow to catch birds and too small to take on narwhals or other whales.

Over the water comes the smell of walrus—not typical polar bear prey. Nanu isn't large enough to kill a full-grown walrus, male or female. But if Nanu could sneak up on a youngster or a sick and weakened walrus . . . that would be a fine meal.

Perched on a melting berg, Nanu is forced to make a decision: Stay on the ice remnants where she can't find food or follow the scent of prey into the unknown sea?

Cautiously, Nanu lowers herself into the sea. She has decided.

For a full week, night and day, the herd travels. It's a 200-mile (300-kilometer) swim. All the walruses are exhausted, but the journey is especially hard on the young and the old.

Walruses can live up to 40 years, and several cows in the herd are approaching that age. The old ones' whiskers are gray, their skin is wrinklier and more mottled even than their younger companions' skin, and their tusks are worn down to stubs.

Seela is young and energetic, but she's smaller than the adult walruses. She's got a smaller store of fat to draw energy from. The long swim wears her out. If the herd doesn't reach its destination soon, Seela will have to give up.

Seela's mother and Auntie urge her on with gentle nudges and reassuring grunts.

Meanwhile, Nanu too is growing tired. She paddles steadily, following the herd's scent over the open sea.

Her fat and fur keep her warm even after days of swimming in the cold water. But like Seela, there's only so long Nanu can survive in the open water. If she doesn't find someplace to haul out, she'll become exhausted and drown.

Above her, Nanu hears a squawking call, and then another. She looks up. A pair of Ross's gulls circle and dip overhead. And where there are gulls, ice—or land—must be near.

Finally the walrus herd reaches its destination: Rock Island. No ice here, but at least the herd can haul out of the ocean and rest on the rocky shore.

But for a walrus, hauling out onto rock is more difficult than clambering onto an ice floe. It's easier to slide forward using tusks to grip slippery ice than it is to lift 2,000 pounds (1,000 kg) of blubber using only the strength of flippers.

Still, the walruses set upon the task immediately. They are tired, and the sooner they're up on the rocks, the sooner they can take a much-needed break.

Auntie shows Seela the way, attacking the rocks fearlessly. She flops onto a boulder, slides back a little, then lifts herself with her flippers and lunges forward. Her blubber ripples as she hunches along like a gigantic caterpillar. Little by little she hauls herself up onto the rock.

In the water, Seela barks. The waves crash on the rocks, throwing salt spray high into the air. Seela waits for a swell to lift her up and forward, then paddles furiously with her front flippers and lunges onto the rock next to Auntie.

Seela slides down the slippery, seaweed-covered rock back into the surf.

Nearby, Seela's mother has pulled up onto a boulder. She barks in encouragement.

Seela waits for another swell to come along, to give it another try.

On the far side of Rock Island, another animal lies sunning on a rock—a male polar bear who swam ashore the day before.

Like Nanu, the male polar bear had been unable to catch any seals on the slushy, broken-up ice shelf. He swam into open waters in a desperate search for prey.

After resting to recover from the long ocean swim, the male polar bear stirs. He yawns, sniffing the air. He's hungry— starving, in fact.

Walruses aren't a polar bear's preferred prey. They're big, they have dangerous tusks, and they can fight back. Any polar bear would rather hunt a helpless plump little seal. But the male polar bear has little choice now.

He sniffs the wind. He catches the scent of the walrus herd, just now coming ashore on the far side of the island. Shaking his shaggy white coat, the polar bear sets out in their direction.

Nanu paddles relentlessly on, following the cries of the gulls overhead. She is very tired—exhausted. If she doesn't pull out of the water soon, she will drown.

On the horizon in front of her, she sees a

flash of white. A small patch of ice.

Swimming faster now, Nanu makes for the ice, her nose cutting through the water like the prow of a ship.

In minutes she's alongside the icy life raft. Digging her sharp claws into the ice, she pulls herself up onto it. She lies down, bone weary. She's hungry, but more than that, she's sleepy. Walruses can sleep while float-ing, but polar bears can't nap in the water.

Closing her eyes, she falls asleep.

Seela suns herself on her broad flat granite perch. The tide has gone out, and she and the rest of the walrus herd are resting comfortably on the rocky shore.

Nearby, Auntie snorts and snuffles in her

sleep, then lolls onto her back. Her flippers twitch as if she's dreaming of the long swim just completed.

Meanwhile, Seela's mother keeps watch over the herd. They are in a strange, un-friendly place, unlike the familiar pack ice and floes they occupied in years past. Walruses, not exactly nimble on ice, are even less so on rough, hard rock.

Seela's mother sniffs the breeze. Salt spray, the odors of the herd, birds, seaweed. No danger. She barks and rests her head on Seela's flank. She closes her eyes.

The male polar bear picks his way across the rocks that hug the coastline of the little island, following the scent of walrus.

Behind him, at a safe distance, trails an arctic fox. For much of the year, arctic foxes that live on the ice sheet have snow-white fur, to blend in with their surroundings. This fox, who lives among rocks and low scrub brush, has brownish fur.

The fox takes a brief detour from following the bear to pick his way along a steep rock face. Murres nest there, and the fox visits the cliffside colony often, in search of eggs and babies.

Nose down, sniffing at the ground, the fox daintily picks his way along the rocks. One slip, and the fox would tumble hundreds of feet onto the boulders and waves below. But arctic foxes are very surefooted, and the little fox soon nears a murre nest.

The nest consists of a narrow rock ledge—no bed of twigs, leaves, straw, or any other soft material. When murres lay eggs, they do so directly on the hard rock. The babies hatch, grow, and mature, all the while exposed directly to the wind and rain.

The fledgling murre in this nest is nearly old enough to learn to fly. And for a murre, the only way to learn to fly is to dive out into the unknown.

The fox noses carefully up to the nest.

Seeing the fox, the father murre squawks in alarm. The fledgling shuffles along the ledge, trying to escape the fox.

The fox gets ready to pounce. He has to be careful in catching the fledgling not to tumble off the ledge.

The father murre, seeing that the fox is about to spring, knocks the fledgling off the ledge, then dives off after him. Sensing a disturbance, the entire colony of murres, thousands of birds, takes flight. The flock wheels in a circle over the sea.

Plummeting through the air, the fledgling flaps its wings awkwardly. It's not strong enough to really fly yet. It smacks into the sea at a faster speed than a more experienced murre would have—and immediately bobs to the surface. Its father lights on the water beside it.

Shaken but unharmed, the fledgling has learned two valuable lessons: first, flying may not be easy, but it's not impossible. And second, foxes are the enemy.

Frustrated by the fledgling's escape, the little fox scampers back up the rock face. He isn't dependent on polar bears for his food the way the foxes on the ice sheet are. There are plenty of birds and other small animals on Rock Island for the fox to hunt.

Nevertheless, the prospect of dining on a polar bear's leftovers keeps him trotting along after the male bear.

Waking after a long, restful sleep, Nanu stretches and yawns. She's no longer so tired, but she's as hungry as ever.

She sees birds circling on the horizon—a sure sign of land. She sniffs at the wind coming from the direction of the birds. Walrus.

Nanu leaps off the ice and into the sea, following the scent.

CHAPTER SIX

The summer sun beats down on Rock Island, raising the temperatures above 50 degrees Fahrenheit (10 degrees Celsius).

Walruses laze in the heat. Their blubbery bodies spread out, almost seeming to melt in the sun.

When a walrus has spent hours in cold water, the tiny vessels that take blood to the skin contract, leaching the skin of blood and giving the animal a pale, ghostly appearance.

But in the hot summer sun, the blood vessels to the skin enlarge, bringing blood to the surface. Blood circulating in the skin helps to cool the walrus down and gives the animal a reddish-brown appearance.

Walruses are covered over most of their bodies with short bristly hair. The bottoms of their flippers are hairless, and of course the hair on their faces—their mustaches—is much longer.

Although quite thick and tough—the skin on the neck is more than an inch thick—walrus skin is very sensitive. Salt from seawater lodges in the minute wrinkles of the walruses' skin. The tiny salt crystals irritate the skin, which is already pink and tender from the sun. Hoping for a blood meal, blackflies swarm the herd, biting the animals.

The itching begins.

Seela scratches her belly with a flipper. Her mother grinds her neck against a satisfyingly sharp outcrop of rock. Auntie stretches and turns, trying to get at an itchy spot between her eyes. She rubs her forehead against Seela's side. Relief for both of them!

All through the herd, walruses scratch themselves and each other to relieve the itchiness brought on by the midday sun.

Nanu swims toward Rock Island. The smell of walrus gives her strength.

The arctic fox leaps from boulder to boulder, swishing his large, bushy tail back and forth for balance. He's followed the male polar bear from one side of Rock Island to the other.

The male bear can hear the walruses braying and barking on the rocks below him. He's uncertain how to hunt a walrus. His usual hunting methods—waiting patiently and motionlessly by a seal's breathing hole, or pouncing on a seal in its icy burrow— don't apply here. He can't sneak up on the walruses. And walruses, with their long sharp tusks, can fight back.

The polar bear is hungry, but he hesitates.

The arctic fox whines and yips quietly to himself. He's hungry too.

Restless from the hot sun, Seela clambers up the rocky beach. Like any walrus, she moves slowly and laboriously over land. But her flippers are strong, and with effort, she is able to climb part of the way along a precarious ledge.

Sea gulls and terns nervously flap about, and high above, a peregrine falcon circles lazily, riding a thermal draft. An arctic ground squirrel darts among the rocks, trying to avoid the falcon's gaze.

Seela's mother and Auntie doze peacefully on the rocks below. They are unaware of the danger that Seela is about to encounter.

The male bear creeps toward the walrus herd, looking for a youngster that would be easy to kill. Failing that, the bear would take an older or a sick animal, or one that has been injured.

The ancestor of the polar bear is the brown, or grizzly, bear. About 200,000 years ago, populations of brown bears in what is now Canada, northern Europe, and Siberia became stranded on ice floes, which drifted north to the Arctic. These populations of bears managed to survive in the harsh climate of the far north. By about a 100,000 years ago, the descendents of those bears had evolved into modern-day polar bears.

Though polar bears prefer ice and water, and brown bears prefer solid ground, the two species are closely related to each other. In fact, polar bears and grizzly bears **are known to have mated and produced** offspring.

This polar bear is strong, fully mature, and not yet beginning to age—in the prime of life. He will never be more able to take on difficult prey like a walrus. And he may never again be so desperate.

Seela's mother awakes. She looks around her. She sees Auntie, asleep with her flipper resting over her head to shade her eyes from the sun.

Where is Seela?

Seela's mother barks, calling for her.

No answer.

Seela's mother barks again, and again no answer comes.

The barking wakes up Auntie, who immediately joins Seela's mother in calling for Seela.

Out of sight of her aunt and mother, and out of earshot too, on a narrow rocky ledge, Seela whimpers in distress.

It's difficult for a walrus to pull herself up a rocky slope—but it's impossible for her to climb down.

Seela has managed to wedge herself into a spot she can't get out of. She can't move forward—the ledge becomes too narrow. She can't move up—there's a sheer rock face that rises straight up beside her. And she can't back along the ledge, either—walruses simply aren't that nimble.

There's nowhere to go but straight down, off the sheer cliff and onto the rocks below.

Fifteen feet (5 meters) down, the surf crashes into a narrow crack between granite outcroppings. The seawater surges up, then quickly drains away to leave bare rock. Then back into the crack the sea flows—back and forth, back and forth, back and forth.

Seela twists her head around, trying to see if there's some way out of this situation. She barks pitifully. There isn't. And the situation is getting worse.

Seela spots the male polar bear not 50 feet (15 meters) away. He's coming toward her.

And she's trapped.

Auntie and Seela's mother bark frantically, but Seela doesn't answer. They don't know where she is, and they don't know what kind of danger she's in either.

The male polar bear moves in for the kill. The walrus stuck on the ledge has her back toward him, and she won't be able to turn around to face him with her tusks.

He trots toward her, head lowered, readying his attack.

Seela has only one option. Without looking, she throws her weight into the air, tumbling awkwardly off the ledge.

Luckily, the surf has just come in, and she hits water rather than rock.

Stunned, she momentarily gets swept up in the surging seawater. She rolls in the water, helpless. But she quickly comes to her senses and squirms to regain her proper orientation. She beats her flippers and brings her tail down hard, propelling herself out of the narrow crack between rock faces and into the open sea.

Angry that his prey has escaped, the polar bear roars. He's desperate now. He must find something to eat, and soon.

CHAPTER SEVEN

A clear blue sky arches over Rock Island. The walrus herd is massed on the flat black granite rocks that tumble down into the sea. Dozens of walruses lounge about, draped on top of one another, some nuzzling whiskers, some snoring, some grunting irritably in the heat. They scratch and belch, yawn and fart.

To a polar bear, they are a tempting, though dangerous, meal.

The male polar bear, driven by extreme hunger, takes the direct approach. He quickly descends the rocky slope. Before the walruses can even react, he is upon them.

But the walruses are bigger than he is. He can't simply leap on one, as he would with a little ringed seal, and bite its head and neck, killing it instantly. Tough walrus skin and the six-inch layer of blubber beneath it further protects the animal's vital organs. And those tusks can rip through polar bear fur.

The bear is right next to the herd, but he doesn't know what to do. The walruses are aware of him now, and they bark in panic and fear. The alarm spreads through the entire herd, which immediately moves, together, toward the sea. Flopping and heaving, the walruses make a mad rush down the rocks to get into the water.

Cautiously, the polar bear pursues the herd. He isn't really committed to the hunt, and when one of the walruses closest to him wheels around and jabs at him with her tusks, he backs away. The walrus bellows angrily and lunges toward him, and the bear turns and skips away. On land, he's much quicker and more agile than she is. She gives up the pursuit, wheels around, and caterpillars quickly down the rock slope and into the sea.

The bear knows better than to follow the walrus into the sea. When a walrus and a polar bear fight in the ocean, the walrus swims circles around the bear, using her tusks as swords to stab the bear in the belly. Such fights usually end in serious injury, or even death, for the bear.

Dejected, famished, the bear climbs back up the rocky bluff.

Seela glides through the water. On land she is awkward and clumsy, but here, in her native element, she is graceful, almost elegant in her movement. Her ribs are sore from her hard landing in the shallow water, but she is uninjured.

Next to her swim her mother and Auntie. The other members of the herd bob nearby, barking to one another, making sure that everyone is accounted for.

Although the bear failed in his hunt, the herd is unwilling to return to the part of the island they'd just been chased from.

There is no single leader of a walrus

herd. In this case, the herd decides, all together, to swim around Rock Island to find a new landing place.

Nanu is a solitary animal—she makes all her decisions by herself. She has successfully followed the cries of birds and the scent of prey to Rock Island. She is hungry and alone, with no one to care for or help her.

She pads across a rough boulder, seaweed squishing between her toes. The environment of Rock Island is so different from the one she has grown up in. There is no ice here, no snow. The air is warm and smells of vegetation and rotting shellfish and bird droppings. The colors are brown and green and gray, not white. There is no sharp tang of ice in the air.

Nanu is desperately hungry, but there are no ringed seals on Rock Island. Murres are no easier to catch here than they were on the ice, and besides, she'd have to catch dozens of the little birds in order to fill her belly. The other little creatures that live on the island—squirrels, voles, lemmings, hares—are far too quick for her to catch. And again, even if she did manage to catch one, it would hardly make a mouthful, let alone a meal.

Nanu scans the scene before her. Murres dive into the sea, catching fish. Out at sea a bowhead whale spouts, a V-shaped spray shooting 20 feet (6 meters) into the air. The whale lifts its white lower jaw out of the water, then slides back under the surface. Blackflies buzz around Nanu's ears.

Nanu sniffs at the low-growing vegetation at her feet—mosses and lichens mostly.

Nearby a tenacious rock willow only 6 inches (15 centimeters) in height is rooted to a bit of soil lodged in the crack between two rocks. Nanu licks at the willow's leaves, then takes a nibble.

Unlike their cousins the brown bear, which eat a wide variety of plants as well as animals, polar bears have evolved to survive on a strictly carnivorous diet.

Nanu spits out the nasty-tasting leaf. She must find meat.

Following the scent of walrus, Nanu sets out to walk the short distance across Rock Island.

Seela and the walrus herd have found a new beach on the other side of the island.

It is already occupied by a large herd of walruses, however. Seela's herd must convince the other herd to make room.

Auntie is the first onto the rocky beach, barking and growling to establish her right to a space. The dominant members of the other herd bark and bellow at her, but they give way. Auntie is determined.

Seela's mother and the other adults from the herd go ashore, as the rival herd clears a space on the rocks for them. Then Seela, too, flops up onto the rocks.

It is a good place to rest. There is plenty of food in the deep water off the shore, as evidenced by the thousands of empty clam shells washed up among the rocks. Seela's herd can share this part of Rock Island for the remainder of the summer and wait for the pack ice to re-form in the fall.

In the ocean, no more than half a mile away from Seela's herd, the male bear paddles relentlessly toward shore.

Although he failed to take a walrus in his first attempt, the male bear has had little choice but to follow the herd—out to sea, and now back to land again, at this new part of Rock Island.

The bear can hear the walrus herds fussing at each other. He dives down, pulling his body swiftly through the water with his large, paddle-like paws.

Traveling overland, Nanu has reached the walrus herds. She gazes down on them from a rocky outcropping hundreds of feet above them. From here the walruses look small and harmless—like seals. They don't smell like seals, but Nanu is hungry—her stomach aches, and she feels weak. The walruses smell enough like prey to pull her forward, down the rock cliff.

Nanu isn't nearly full grown yet. She's less than half the size of the male polar bear, and she's not nearly as experienced a hunter. And even he was unable to kill one of the herd when he had a chance.

Timidly, Nanu approaches. One of the walruses spots her and bawls in anger. The walrus shakes her head and rears back, flashing her tusks and appearing to grow even larger.

Nanu whimpers. With no real plan, she darts forward, hoping that somehow she can kill the monster.

The walrus lashes out with her tusks, braying. Several other big females rush forward to join in her defense. They roar and snarl angrily.

Nanu yelps and skips aside, dodging the deadly tusks. Turning tail, she scampers up the rocky slope to safety.

Her last chance at a kill seems to be no chance at all. Has she come all this way only to starve?

CHAPTER EIGHT

The male bear doesn't give up so easily. The warm summer sun shines down on the walruses on the beach. They are drowsy with the heat. Seela dozes, stretched out with her hind flippers on her mother and her muzzle wedged into her Auntie's side. Seela's mother and Auntie, usually so vigilant, ready for anything, are sleeping, too. After all, it's been an especially exhausting morning.

The breeze blows out from shore. The walrus herd doesn't smell the polar bear approaching from the sea.

The bear climbs out of the water and charges into the herd, taking the walruses by surprise. This time he is so desperate for a kill that he is willing to risk being slashed by their tusks.

Alarmed, the walruses scatter, shrieking. The herds stampede in the direction of the sea. For the second time that day, Auntie and Seela's mother run for their lives, heaving themselves as fast as they can toward the safety of the water.

Seela tries to follow them, but before she can move, the polar bear is upon her.

On a rocky ledge above, Nanu witnesses the male bear's attack. She sniffs the wind and growls hungrily.

Desperately Seela writhes and twists, trying to throw the bear off her. She lunges at him with her tusks. But she is young, and her tusks are not yet the long, swordlike weapons the older walruses possess.

The bear grips her shoulders with his paws and gnaws at the back of her neck, trying to plunge his sharp canine teeth into her flesh.

Seela screams in terror.

Nanu begins to make her way down the
cliff. There will be meat. One way or the
other, Nanu must have some.

Behind her, a fox pricks up its ears. It
follows her down the rocks.

Seela's mother plunges into the sea and,
in a panic, dives to the bottom. All around
her, frightened walruses dart through
the water.

Auntie is about to follow Seela's mother
into the waves, but pulls up short. A young
walrus is screaming—Auntie recognizes the
voice. It is Seela's.

Auntie turns and charges back up the rock. She sees the polar bear clinging to Seela's back. She hurls herself at the pair, slashing at the white fur of the bear with her tusks.

Auntie and the bear roll over each other, slamming into the sharp face of a boulder.

Freed from her attacker, Seela humps as fast as she can for the sea. In seconds she's at the water's edge, and she dives in.

CHAPTER NINE

S eela dives to the bottom of the sea. The cold water soothes the gashes on her shoulder and neck. Her wounds aren't life threatening. They will heal soon enough.

Surfacing, she gives a calling bark. Her mother barks in reply, and the two walruses find each other amid the many bobbing heads of the herd. Seela and her mother press their muzzles together, blowing air into each other's faces. They touch each other with their sensitive whiskers.

Reassured to have found each other, they call out for Auntie.

Seela barks and rumbles. Her mother barks too. Repeatedly they call out for Auntie, pausing periodically to listen for a reply.

But Auntie doesn't answer.

The sun is setting. The long summer is ending. The herd is moving once again to find a part of Rock Island where there are no polar bears.

In the east, the moon rises low on the horizon. To the north, the aurora borealis— a shifting, multicolored curtain of light— reflects off the sea.

Seela's mother has stopped calling for Auntie. But Seela hasn't. She barks, over and over again.

She doesn't hear any answer.

Her mother will stay with Seela until she gives up, and then the two will rejoin the herd. But for now, Seela barks, hoping for a reply that will never come.

CHAPTER TEN

The sun is rising. Nanu is growing weak. Without food, she can't last much longer.

Nanu spent the night on the rocky beach, loitering around the male bear and his kill.

The male bear, eating slowly but methodically, would growl whenever Nanu came too near. Polar bears are not in the habit of sharing even when, as in this case, there's more meat than a single bear can possibly consume.

The male bear had been desperate enough for food to brave a full-grown walrus's tusks. Nanu is now desperate enough to brave a full-grown polar bear's claws and fangs.

Nanu sidles up to the male bear. He growls low in his throat, threatening to attack, but Nanu won't give in. She darts forward bravely and tries to rip a piece of flesh from the carcass.

The male bear roars and charges at her. The fur along the back of his neck is on end, and his angry snarl reveals his long, sharp canines.

Nanu squeals and scampers away. But she doesn't go far, and soon she's right back. She must share in the kill.

Nanu tries to take another quick bite, and once again the male bear chases her off. His hair doesn't stand on end this time, though, and his snarl is less fierce. His belly is full, he's very sleepy, and it just may not be worth his trouble to defend his kill against this little intruder.

The male bear growls at Nanu, but she stands her ground.

Lowering her body in a gesture of subservience, Nanu approaches the kill. The male bear grunts, but he makes no move toward her. She nibbles at the carcass. Then she relaxes and begins to feast. The walrus meat is fatty and nutritious.

The male bear walks away to lie down on a flat sunning rock. He needs to sleep off his meal.

Nanu feeds greedily. Up the slope, the little fox twitches his nose, waiting patiently. His turn will come.

A single death preserves the lives of many.

CHAPTER ELEVEN

For each of the next four years, Nanu
and Seela are driven to this rocky out-
post as the pack ice melts earlier and earlier.

Due to global climate changes caused
by release of carbon dioxide gas into the
atmosphere, summer sea ice in the Arctic
has declined by 30 percent over the last half
century. Temperatures in different parts of
the Arctic have risen three to five degrees.
The last time the Arctic was so warm was

125,000 years ago—before polar bears had evolved into a distinct species from brown bears. The best computer models estimate that if current trends continue, by the end of this century temperatures will rise by another eight degrees. Pack ice will be a thing of the past. So might the polar bear and the walrus.

But for now, the ice sheet still forms over the northern ocean.

In the spring of her eighth year, Nanu seeks out the companionship of male bears for the first time. She is ready to mate. When she finds a likely looking male, she spends a week with him. For that brief time, the pair are inseparable. They wander across the ice, hunting seals together. When the week of mating is over, the bears separate. Probably they'll never see each other again.

In the fall, for the first time since she was a cub, Nanu interrupts her life of roaming. She returns to Snow Mountain and, like her mother before her, digs a den in the icy slope. There she will curl up and sleep for four months.

By Seela's eighth year, her tusks have filled out nicely. Seela, too, is ready to mate.

Her all-female herd is serenaded throughout the winter by male walruses eager to impress them with the complexity and sophistication of their songs. The males whistle and cluck, display their tusks, and do battle with their male rivals, all in the hopes of being chosen by the females.

When the females decide collectively that a male has won their favor, they allow him to join the herd. The male has exclusive access to the females for one to five days, mating with as many of them as he can in that period.

After his time is up, the females eject him from the herd. They then invite another singer to join them.

By late winter, Seela is carrying a growing calf in her womb. She will be pregnant for over a year before giving birth.

On Snow Mountain, where she was born, Nanu produces a miracle of the north—twin miracles, in fact, a girl and a boy, just like her mother before her. Nanu, too, sleeps through the birth itself.

The tiny blind newborn pups creep slowly along Nanu's belly in a quest for nourishment. They find the nipple and nurse.

Nanu will dedicate the next two years of her life to caring for her precious cubs.

When spring comes, Seela delivers a miracle of her own—a newborn calf, sleek and bold, an expert swimmer from the first hours of life.

There's a new Auntie, too—not for Seela, but for her calf. Seela and her baby's Auntie will spend the next two years guarding Seela's calf as it grows.

All across the Arctic, plants and animals wake anew each spring. Foxes, seals, and murres. Sedges, mosses, and grasses. Whales and narwhals, mice and squirrels. Even clams and blackflies. All form part of the complex, interdependent web of life, as they have for thousands of years.

Their fates are forever tied to the shifting rhythms of the ice that defines them, to the blanket of cold that keeps this kingdom theirs.